WILLIAM BOLCOM

SEVEN EASY PIANO PIECES

ISBN 978-1-4234-2496-3

EDWARD B.
MARKS MUSIC
COMPANY

Exclusively Distributed By

HAL•LEONARD®
CORPORATION

7777 W. BLUEMOUND RD. P.O. BOX 13819 MILWAUKEE, WI 53213

Visit Hal Leonard Online at
www.halleonard.com

TABLE OF CONTENTS

FOREWORD

A couple decades ago, my wife Joan Morris began to take piano lessons with Sarah Albright, whose late husband William Albright was one of the last century's greatest organist-composers. Joan loves cats, whence the three Pussycat Waltzes.

WB (December, 2009)

for my wife, Joan Morris

SEVEN EASY PIANO PIECES
1. Pussycat Waltz No. 1

William Bolcom

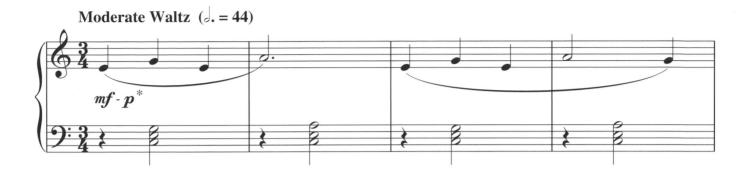

*1st time **mf**, 2nd time **p**

N.B. Metronome markings are not absolute.

2. Winter Trek

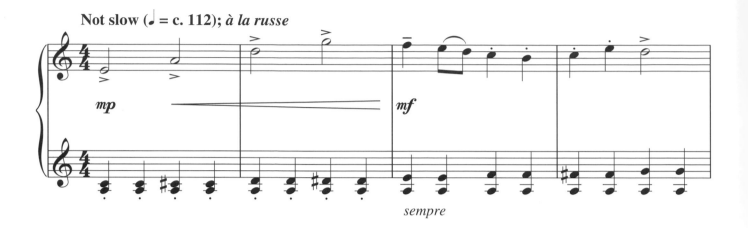

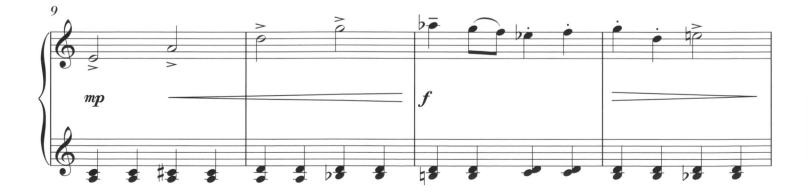

una corda

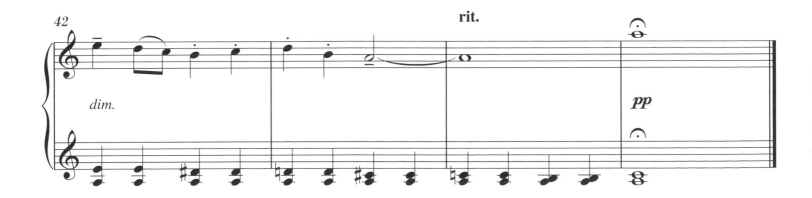

This page is left blank to facilitate page turns.

3. Little Song

Andante moderato (♩ = c. 69); *teneramente*

p smooth | *& expressive*

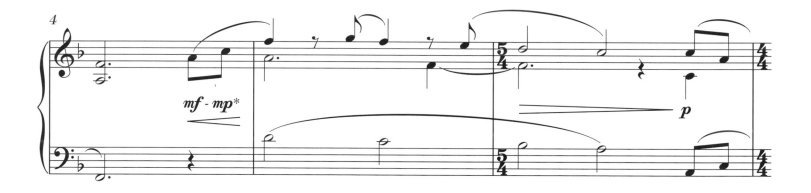

*mf - mp**

p

pp

mp

*1st time **mf**, 2nd time **mp***

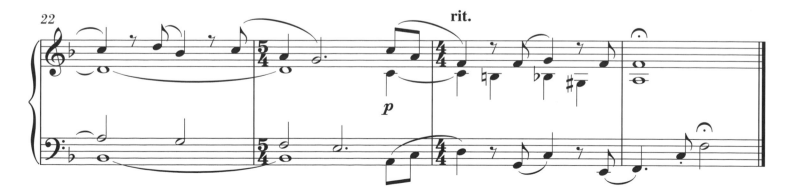

4. Pussycat Waltz No. 2

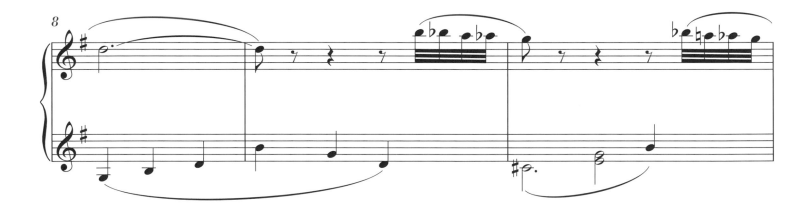

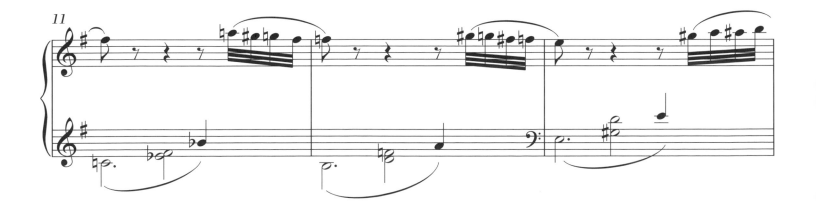

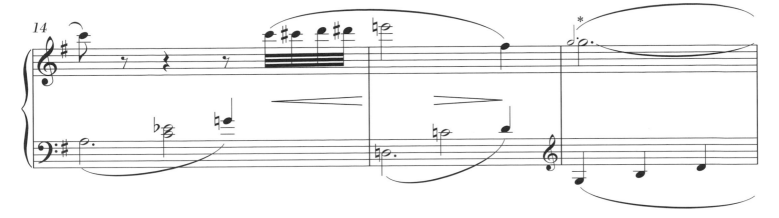

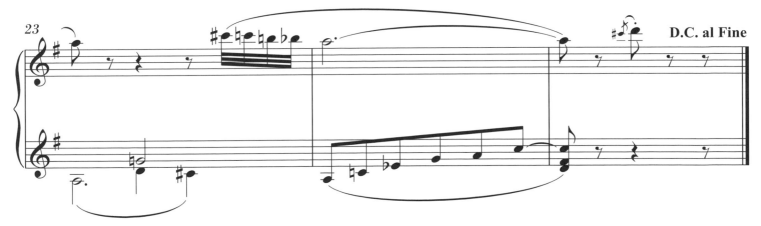

*play small notes last time.

5. Little French Invention: *L'Orangerie*

Moderato (♩ = 90); *with dignity*

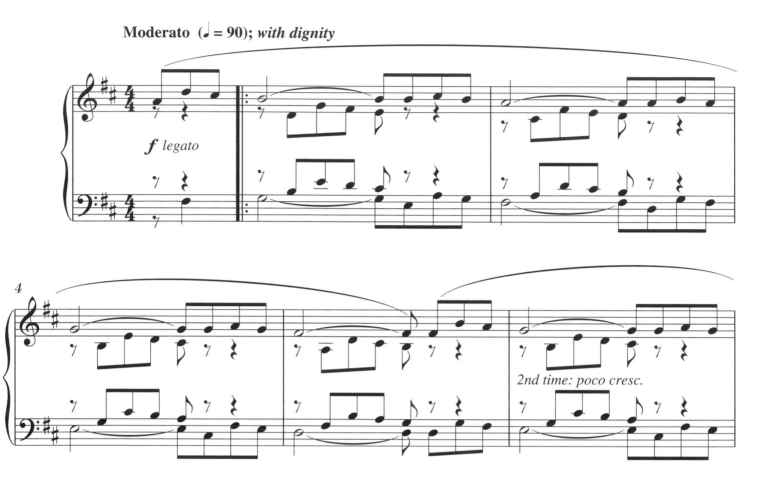

f legato

2nd time: poco cresc.

1.

molto rit.

2.

p

mp

cresc. molto

ff

6. Carillon

Not slow (♩ = 100)

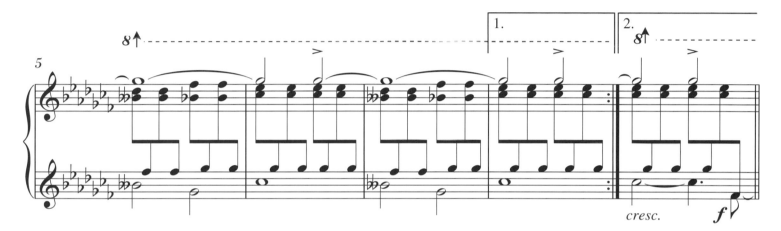

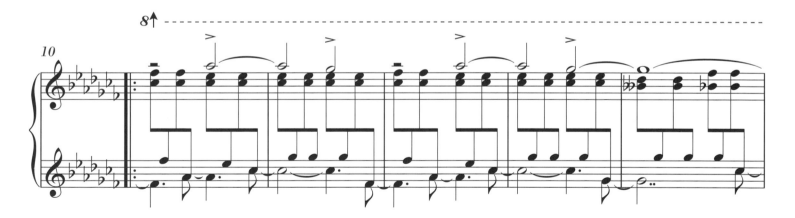

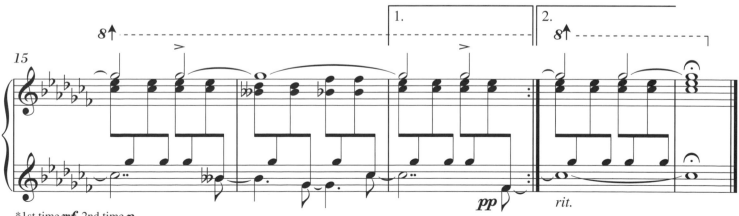

*1st time **mf**, 2nd time **p**

C♭ Major: The only 3 notes here on white keys are C♭, B♭♭ and F♭.

7. Pussycat Waltz No. 3

Not fast (♩. = 40); *graceful*

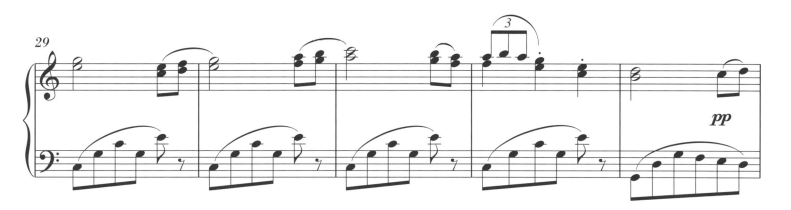

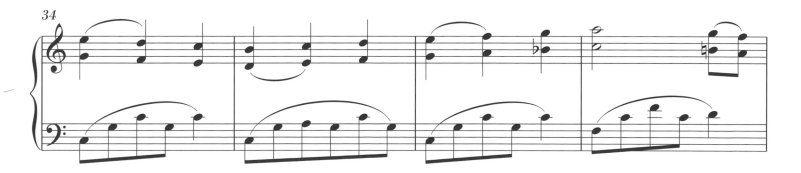

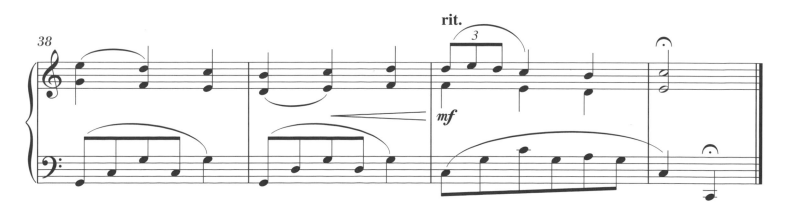